BRITANNIA
TRIUMPHANS

THIS IS THE TWELFTH OF THE

WALTER NEURATH MEMORIAL LECTURES

WHICH ARE GIVEN ANNUALLY EACH SPRING ON

SUBJECTS REFLECTING THE INTERESTS OF

THE FOUNDER

OF THAMES AND HUDSON

THE DIRECTORS WISH TO EXPRESS

PARTICULAR GRATITUDE TO THE GOVERNORS AND

MASTER OF BIRKBECK COLLEGE

UNIVERSITY OF LONDON

FOR THEIR GRACIOUS SPONSORSHIP OF

THESE LECTURES

BRITANNIA TRIUMPHANS

INIGO JONES
RUBENS
AND
WHITEHALL PALACE

ROY STRONG

THAMES AND HUDSON

Printed in Great Britain by BAS Printers Limited, Over Wallop, Hampshire
Bound in Great Britain by Webb and Sons

I never had the good fortune to know Walter Neurath. The books he produced were amongst those which, when I was a schoolboy and student after the Second World War, first excited my interest in the history of the visual arts. Anyone who experienced this excitement after a childhood of visual starvation can only feel gratitude to the memory of a man who contributed so signally to the post-war renaissance in art books. Now his successors lavish the same care and imagination on the work of a new generation of scholars, including myself. Walter Neurath was keenly interested in the interdisciplinary approach to the history of the visual arts, epitomized by the work of Aby Warburg and his successors, which has so enriched our understanding of the whole European tradition. It has also revolutionized the study of British art, too long the victim of backwater parochialism. I hope that this reconsideration of the Whitehall Banqueting House and its ceiling, an extended version of the Memorial Lecture, would have intrigued him, because as long ago as 1957 he published the first significant study of the subject by Per Palme. One thing his mind was clearly never closed to was the airing of new ideas on old problems.

1 Van Dyck, *Inigo Jones*

IN THE AUTUMN of 1637 Charles I's Surveyor of Works, Inigo Jones, was busy supervising the erection of a temporary room in Whitehall Palace. All through the winter months a team of workmen laboured to create this new hall, one which in modern terms we would refer to as a theatre, but which was called at the time the masquing room, built in haste to accommodate the King's New Year masque, *Britannia Triumphans*. In this Charles I was presented as the god-appointed ruler Britanocles, issuing from a Palace of Fame, with open allusions to the naval power achieved through the imposition of the hated Ship Money tax, the case for which was being tried simultaneously in the courts. On the occasion of the judges' pronouncement in favour of the Crown the court celebrated its victory by a second masque, composed in six weeks, *Luminalia, or the Festival of Light*. This time it was Charles's unpopular Queen, Henrietta Maria, who danced a ballet expressing the defeat of the opposition in the purest Neoplatonic terms of darkness banished by light.[1] Thus the Stuart court resumed its recondite revels after an interruption of some three years.

The reason for the interruption was that it had no longer been practical to use the hall built for the purpose, Inigo Jones's Whitehall Banqueting House, which, as the combination of ceremonial hall and *salle des fêtes*, was the most important room in the palace. Sir William Davenant, who wrote the texts of both masques, explains in *Britannia Triumphans* how 'the room where formerly they were presented having the ceiling since richly adorned with pieces of painting of great value figuring the acts of King James of happy memory, and other enrichments; lest this might suffer by the smoke of many lights, his majesty commanded . . . a new temporary room'.[2] In this way the masque text contains the first public reference to the famous series of canvases by Peter Paul Rubens, apart from the Banqueting House itself the single most important artistic commission by the English Crown in the first half of the seventeenth century.

2 *The Palace of Fame in 'Britannia Triumphans'*

3 *Costume for Charles I in 'Britannia Triumphans'*

Inigo Jones's designs
for the royal masques for 1637

4 *Transformation scene in 'Luminalia'*

5 *Costume for Henrietta Maria in 'Luminalia'*

6 *The Whitehall Banqueting House. The view from the throne*

INIGO JONES AND INVENTION

The historical facts concerning the ceiling are remarkably few. Sixteen years before, in 1621, at the end of a letter from Rubens to the English agent in Brussels, William Trumbull, the artist adds a postscript: 'As for his Majesty and His Royal Highness the Prince of Wales, I shall always be very much pleased to receive the honour of their commands; and regarding the hall in the new palace, I confess that I am, by natural instinct, better fitted to execute very large works than small curiosities.'[3] To his surprising allusion to a 'new palace' I shall return later, but this is the first reference that we have to an approach by James I and Prince Charles to Rubens to paint the Banqueting House ceiling. Eight years were to pass until the summer of 1628, when Rubens was employed to assist in the negotiations for a treaty between Charles I and Philip IV of Spain. The painter was in England from 5 June 1629 to 3 March 1630, a period of some seven months, and was entirely successful in his mission. On 11 January Don Carlos de Coloma, the Spanish Ambassador,

10

8 Rubens, *Self-portrait*   9 Rubens, *Preliminary sketch for the ceiling (detail)*

made his public entry into London and on 15 December a treaty of peace was signed. Rubens returned to the Low Countries with a knighthood, besides being laden with costly presents. Silence then falls until, in August 1634, Balthasar Gerbier, writing from Brussels, refers to the gossip of those who visited the painter's studio concerning 'the great works he hath made for the banqueting house' which 'lye in his [house] as arrested for want of money to call him and the said works into England'. A year later Rubens resigned himself to doing what he could to them in his studio 'in terms as shall not need to be retouched when sett in their place'.[4] Later in the autumn the canvases were on their way, although the artist was not paid for them until June 1638 when, along with a gold chain by way of compensation, he finally received £3,000.

These are the known historical facts. To them we can add a series of studies of the ceiling, all of which save one belong to the 1940s and 1950s, by Fritz Saxl, Donald Gordon, Per Palme and Oliver Millar.[5]

The most recent of all has been Julius Held's important article of 1970 on the positioning of the canvases, based on a reconsideration of Rubens's preliminary sketch for the ceiling at Glynde.[6] Working from a study of court etiquette and from his knowledge of Venetian ceiling paintings of the same type, Held has established what was without doubt the true orientation of the panels, a discovery which became fact when the Banqueting House was recently restored and the pictures repositioned. And it is this which first prompted me to reopen the subject of the iconography of the ceiling, for the relocation of the panels must have implications for its meaning. In addition, a generation has passed since any scholar has attempted an analysis of its subject-matter. Since the 1950s there has been not only a revolution in the study of the form and content of Stuart court festivals but above all a revaluation of the quite extraordinary position occupied by Inigo Jones at the Caroline court.[7] Jones has suffered from the compartmentalization of modern scholarship. Historians of painting discuss the ceiling, historians of architecture the Banqueting House and palace, historians of literature the court masques. But all three are offsprings of the same mind and imagination, that of the court's polymath Vitruvian architect-engineer, Inigo Jones.

What I wish to begin by arguing are the essentially Jonesian roots of the ceiling programme. Transmuted, of course, it inevitably was by the brush of Rubens into the international idiom of the baroque, but there are so many details which Rubens could only have reached by reference to a written programme compiled by someone familiar with the mythology of the Stuart dynasty as it had developed over a period of thirty years. Who was the person or persons who conceived this programme? Oliver Millar favoured Rubens and Charles I; D. J. Gordon, Inigo Jones and Archbishop Laud. The latter was never noted for his interest in the arts and his pronouncements on Divine Monarchy echo those of any number of prelates in the decades down to 1642. Surely the person who drew up the programme can only ever have been Inigo Jones. He designed the building, he alone had been intimately associated with all the masques performed within it, gradually edging out Ben Jonson and claiming for himself the mantle of being sole 'inventor'. We are so used to approaching the masques by means of the literary texts that we forget that it was Jones who actually devised the plots and allegories of virtually all of them after 1630.

In the recent reassessment of the masques,[8] Jones emerges as the key figure working in direct consultation with the King, who took a deep interest in the subject-matter of court drama as well as himself being the focal point of the masques. The missing document which would explain the programme of the ceiling would be along the lines of the gloss attached, for example, to the printed text of *Tempe Restored* (1632), for which the verses were written by Aurelian Townshend, but for which it is specifically stated that 'the subject matter and allegory of the masque with the descriptions and apparatus of the scene, were invented by Inigo Jones'.[9] A similar phrase occurs in the published text of the last of the court masques, Davenant's *Salmacida Spolia* (1640): 'The invention, ornament, scenes, and apparitions, with their descriptions, were made by Inigo Jones, Surveyor General of his Majesty's Works'.[10] As Gordon and Millar have pointed out, parts of the proscenium arch decoration for *Salmacida Spolia* are identical to motifs on the ceiling. For these scholars it is significant that Jones is using motifs from the ceiling in the masque which, of course, he was, but surely the real point is that here we have an allegorical programme in the words of Inigo Jones which includes part of the ceiling imagery and its meaning as a natural means of expression. In the words of Gordon: 'As Rubens' ceiling expresses the triumph of Charles's autocracy, *Salmacida Spolia* expresses its tragedy. Ceiling and masque speak a common figurative language, at times revealing a relationship so close as to suggest that Jones and Davenant, composing their entertainment, had the programme of the ceiling before them.'[11] I would suggest that Jones and Davenant did not have the programme before them. They did not need to, for Jones was its author. Jones was merely doing here what he so often did over the years – quote himself.

We have forgotten that it was normal for Jones to put together what was technically categorized as the 'invention'. Ramshackle and derivative these allegorical programmes usually were, if compared with the taut handiwork of a Ben Jonson. And this too applies to the ceiling. It also tends to be ramshackle in its iconographic programme. Although, as I shall demonstrate, there was a central theme, on the whole the programme is a patchwork affair, very much in the vein of Jones's Caroline masques where ideas come and go, where there is a tendency to be discursive and to accumulate incidents of peripheral importance. No doubt the programme was discussed on the spot by Rubens, Jones and the King, but surely no one except the architect could have supplied the artist with the 'invention'. It would have been inconceivable for Jones to have allowed anyone else to develop the schema for his building. The wonder remains that Rubens was able to transmute the programme into a series of paintings that remains the greatest baroque ceiling north of the Alps.

I use the word transmute because I have no doubt that Rubens must have altered whatever scheme was given him. An artist of his international standing and one whom Charles I wanted so desperately would have had a reasonably free rein in the interpretation of his brief. But the fact remains that the Whitehall programme is very different, for instance, from that for the Marie de' Medici cycle. Rubens could never have had the knowledge to have composed such a celebration of the Protestant Kings of Britain. In what follows Rubens to some extent gets lost, for what I am trying to do is to look at the ceiling from the English or Jonesian end. I make no apology for this because I have no doubt that Rubens scholars will in their turn tilt the balance back again.

THE JUDGMENT OF SOLOMON:
JAMES I RECREATES THE EMPIRE OF GREAT BRITAIN
From 1635 onwards Charles I, when enthroned in the Banqueting House, gazed towards three panels which the earliest key to the ceiling, probably early nineteenth-century in date, describes as depicting: '*the* KING on his THRONE Pointing to PRINCE CHARLES *who is* CROWN'D KING [of] SCOTLAND Perfected by MINERVA or WISDOM' flanked by 'HERCULES *Representing* HEROIC VIRTUES Demolishing ENVY' and

10 Rubens, *The Judgment of Solomon: James I recreates the Empire of Great Britain*

'PALLAS *or* MINERVA *Representing* HEROIC CHASTITY Destroying LUST'.[12] Let us begin with the first, the central panel.

In considering this we can reach certain generalizations that apply to the rest of the ceiling, not only in terms of style and mood, but also in those of allegorical theme and content, for the symbolism consists of a carefully interwoven series of motifs stemming from a single common thread. In the first panel James I, crowned and wearing robes of state with the collar of the Order of the Garter, leans forward from a throne set high on a dais beneath a canopy of state rendered as swirling draperies above him. In his left hand he clasps the orb, while with his right he extends his sceptre in a majestic gesture of judgment towards two ladies. These stand to the left on rostra divided by a ravine into which have been piled armour and weapons to which a putto is about to set fire. The bare-breasted maidens, who are England and Scotland, bend towards each other over this chasm, one turning her head in obedient supplication to the King. Between them a child beats down under his feet the weapons of discord while extending a hand to each of the two female figures who support a diadem above his head. The crown is in two parts and a helmeted figure, Minerva or Pallas, ties a knot linking the crowns into one. The tableau in elementary terms is James I commanding the Union of his two kingdoms of England and Scotland into the new Empire of Great Britain. Above, two putti happily celebrate the match, soaring through the air bearing the new arms of the kingdom festooned with a garland of the red and white roses of the houses of York and Lancaster. The whole action takes place within a specific setting, a semi-rotunda with a coffered dome. The King too is attended, to his right, by a man in antique dress and one seated in some kind of court uniform, and, to his left, by two mysterious figures, almost heads only, who gaze in at the action.

The panel celebrates the event of 20 October 1604 when James I proclaimed himself King of Great Britain:[13] '. . . out of undoubted knowledge [we] do use the true and ancient name which God and time have imposed upon this Isle, extant and received in histories, in all maps and cartes wherein this Isle is described . . .' No courtly compliment throughout the reign was complete without some homage to James's staggering achievement of uniting the British Isles under the sovereignty of one imperial diadem.

As Per Palme first pointed out, the composition is based on the Judgment of Solomon. In the First Book of Kings two women contend for a child. Solomon, in his wisdom, decreed that the infant should be divided between them, split in halves. In the ceiling panel the two contending women are England and Scotland, and the judgment of the new Solomon, James I, excels that of his Old Testament predecessor. He reconciles the contestants by commanding the Union of the crowns. The mighty wisdom of this action is emphasized by the sphinx which makes up part of the throne.

The image of James as the new Solomon was his official one, deliberately stressed in his motto *Beati Pacifici*. Daniel Mytens's portrait of

11 Daniel Mytens, *James I (detail)*

him seated beneath a canopy bearing this inscription is typical of many portraits of James in his role as the peace-making Solomon. It is the most all-pervasive of Jacobean themes with a long history stretching back as far as 1579 when, as a child of fourteen, James made his state entry into Edinburgh. On entering the city gate the very first pageant was one of the Judgment of Solomon.[14] As Bishop Montague wrote: 'GOD hath giuen us a Solomon, and God aboue all things gaue Solomon Wisdome; Wisdome brought him peace; Peace brought him Riches'.[15] Forty-six years later in 1625, when Bishop Williams came to deliver the King's funeral oration, it was still on the hackneyed, if resounding, theme of the British Solomon.[16]

This, then, without doubt is the main allusive theme of the ceiling. What is more pertinent is that the story of the famous judgment was applied to the Union by its official apologists. John Thornborough, Bishop of Bristol, moves rapidly through the usual cosmological arguments for the rule of One Monarch to a justification of the Union on just such an analogy:

'. . . let none be so hardie (with the harlot in the daies of Salomon) to say to the King our common parent: Deuide the child, and cut it into two parts; least such diuision part that into two, which God in nature first made one: and now in his greater goodnesse hath restored, in the royall person of our gracious King into one: what God hath so ioyned together, let no man put asunder.'[17]

This vision of the King as a priest effecting a marriage re-echoes James's own words to his first Parliament: 'What God hath conioyned then let no man separate. I am the Husband, and all the whole Isle is my lawful Wife.'[18] And if we return to the ceiling the putto sets fire to the weapons of warfare that divide the kingdoms with a nuptial torch. Jones's gloss when re-using the motif in 1640 is to the point: 'Forgetfulness of Injuries, extinguishing a flaming torch on an armour.'[19]

Who is the child? Palme and Millar accept it as the infant Charles I, but no reason is adduced. Gordon, citing an unpublished lecture by Fritz Saxl, points out that if it were meant to be any particular child it

12 Rubens, *Forgetfulness of Injuries*

would have been Charles's elder brother, Henry, Prince of Wales, who died at eighteen in 1612. Saxl, however, observes:

'The naked child painted in analogy to the Christ child must be an allegorical being representing the happy birth of the United Kingdom. It was James's will – and therefore all eyes are turned towards him – that the Stuarts should, by wisdom's direction, rule over a united island and thus promote eternal peace . . . Thus the . . . picture represents the enthronement of James's successors as the peaceable monarchs of this united island over which Wisdom presides.'[20]

It is an interpretation which I find entirely acceptable.

This scene is enacted within a rotunda with a coffered dome, a circular temple rather than a palace, an architectural image that brought with it the whole range of Renaissance Neoplatonic imagery on the circle and its perfection as an image of God and of a harmonic cosmos. What is more to the point, circular temple imagery in relation to the Union had been used from the very beginning of the reign. In the earliest of the court masques, not so far as we know designed by Jones, the main action centred on a circular Temple of Peace, 'dedicated to Unity and Concord'. Samuel Daniel's *Vision of the Twelve Goddesses* was performed as part of the New Year's revels of 1604 and the masquers were led by Anne of Denmark as Minerva-Pallas, 'the glorious patroness of this mighty Monarchy'.[21] Its climax came when the Goddesses cast themselves into a circle around the Temple while the Graces sang to music played by musicians hidden within its cupola. In symbolic form this was celebrating in the eyes of the court the two major political themes of the moment, 'Concord', the peace negotiations with Spain which were to reach their height in four months time with the arrival of commissioners to treat, and 'Unity', the joining of the two kingdoms under a single crown, a theme upon which James was to elaborate in the Parliament which met two months later. Already in 1604 the Union was expressed in allegorical terms, parallel to those of the ceiling, of a circular temple with the goddess Minerva-Pallas personifying regal wisdom as expressed in heroic action.

The image spills over into official apologies for the Union. Thus, John Thornborough, Bishop of Bristol writes:

'And here let us now consecrate to al eternitie the ancient name of famous great Brittaine, as a Pantheon of al blessings in peace, prosperitie, and honor: for as the Pantheon was a Temple at Rome, round, and like to the capacitie of heaven, wherein were put al the images of their Gods, as in a Pantheon, are placed al worldly blessings, like stars shining from heaven, and having their influence into the whole body of [the] commonweale, even *perfection of beautie in Sion*.'[22]

The natural location of a priest-king was a temple, and in the ideal world of the masque this indeed is where Jones so often places either him or his heir. In the *Masque of Augurs* (1622), which celebrates the *Pax Britannica* of James and prophesies the progeny of Charles and his Spanish bride, the masquers enter from a circular temple based on the Pantheon.[23] Ten years later, in *Albion's Triumph*, Charles, now King, is

22

unveiled as the ideal Platonic ruler before the Temple of Jove attended by priests and sacrificers bearing censers.[24] Where else would a priest-king consecrate a marriage other than within the sacred precincts of a temple?

The religious aura surrounding what we are usually led to regard as a political act draws our attention to a neglected aspect of the Union of the kingdoms. We have seen how the Bishop of Bristol's mind moves naturally on from the Pantheon in Rome to the *'perfection of beautie in*

13 Inigo Jones, *The circular College of Augurs*

Sion', an argument which he develops to include a celebration of James's creation of 'one Ierusalem'. The Anglican Church, of which the King was the theological bastion, depended on the concept of the Ancient British Church which had flourished in these islands centuries before its purity was sullied by the arrival of the popish Augustine and his monks. Christianity, it was accepted, had first been brought to Britain direct from the Holy Land by St Joseph of Arimathea, who lay buried at Glastonbury. King Lucius was the first King to embrace the Christian faith and from Britain sprang the first Christian Emperor, Constantine the Great, born of a British mother. All these were commonplaces in everything written in defence of the Anglican Church in the late sixteenth and seventeenth centuries, whether found in erudite form in Matthew Parker's *De Antiquitate Britannicae Ecclesiae* (1572) or in popular form in John Foxe's *Actes and Monuments* (1563). The accession of James I naturally sent the Anglican apologists into unbounded ecstasies. Union for them was primarily a restoration of the British Church to its ancient unity:

'. . . it is an immortall glorye which shall increase in your raigne, and continue to posterity, seeing your Majesty is the author of the restoring of the true Christian religion in your realmes, hauing restored it I saye to that beauty and sincerity, as it was in the oulde time, planted by *Lucius* your fore-runner, the first Christian King of great *Brittayne* . . .'[25]

James pointing towards the infant is also here in his role as the nursing father of the newly reunited British Church.

The British theme is expanded by the figures grouped to the right and therefore directly associated with the King. With him they look towards the birth of the infant. The first is a man with shaggy hair, seated holding a golden mace. He is wearing a crimson tunic with puffed sleeves banded with black, and on his back there is a Tudor rose and crown. Both Oliver Millar and Donald Gordon believe that this figure must be a Serjeant at Arms, although neither explains why, nor the role such a figure played within the Stuart court.

The only detailed history of the office of Serjeant at Arms is given by Samuel Pegge in his *Curialia* (1806). He states: 'The Serjeants at Arms

. . . were unquestionably the most ancient, and for some centuries the only apparent, Body Guard of our Sovereigns since the Conquest . . .'[26] Although the earliest specific reference to them comes only as late as the reign of Edward II, Pegge has no doubt that they somehow descended from the bodyguard of the Anglo-Saxon and Norman kings. In other words they were the most ancient of the officers of the Royal Household. In the hierarchy of the latter they ranked first, descending thus: Serjeant, Gentleman, Yeoman, Groom and Page. Their most distinctive attribute was a mace which was small enough to be concealed and then suddenly revealed as a symbol of royal authority. Serjeants, therefore, were used in arresting prisoners. As their role declined in the Household, mainly as their arraigning function ceased to be necessary within the legal system, the maces of those that remained grew in size. Elizabeth I had twenty-five Serjeants at Arms, a number which James I, in a fit of economy, reduced to sixteen. From the point of view of the ceiling Jones would have seen them as the ancient bodyguard of the Kings of Britain whose origins were lost in the mists of antiquity. What is more, their dress, like that of the Yeomen of the Guard, had become mummified into that of an earlier era. And this too for Jones had a definite symbolic import.

The dress of the Serjeant at Arms, therefore, belongs neither to the world of antiquity, nor to that of the present, but to the intervening centuries. We can unravel its significance within the British context by elaborating Inigo Jones's views as to what constituted specifically ancient British costume. For Jones in his designs this is always of two types, something he formulated as early as 1611 in Prince Henry's masque of *Oberon*, where the masquers are dressed in the classical style, for the Britons were, of course, part of the antique world, and the torchbearers or other attendants were an approximation to early Tudor court dress.[27] Twenty-five years later he repeated the effect in Thomas Carew's masque *Coelum Britannicum* (1634), whose central theme was the Union of the kingdoms, in which the masquers again were dressed *à l'antique* and the torchbearers in the early Tudor style. And this time the fact is articulated in the masque text, in which it is stated that the torchbearers were dressed in the 'old British fashion'.[28]

14 Rubens, *A Serjeant at Arms*

15 *Masquer in 'Oberon, the Fairy Prince'*

16 *Attendant in 'Oberon, the Fairy Prince'*

Designs by Inigo Jones

17 *Masquer in 'Coelum Britannicum'*

18 *Torchbearer in 'Coelum Britannicum'*

In other words, grouped to the right are figures which across a historical continuum epitomize the ancient Empire of Great Britain. Behind the Serjeant at Arms in his dress of the 'old British fashion' stands a heroic figure, muscular, attired in cuirass and buskins, and with hand on hip. Who is he and what role does he play within the saga? To my mind there can be no doubt that he must be Jones's usual complimentary vision of an ancient Briton, dressed in the classical manner, not one of the earliest and most primitive Britons, who were ruled by Druids and whose uncivilized state was reflected in their wild streaming hair and painted woad adornment, but, as John Speed describes, a 'more civill Britaine'.[29] Although the story of the Trojan descent was under attack in Stuart England, its mythology was repeated even by its opponents, more particularly because of one part of the story that the latter were extremely reluctant to demolish. This was that anchor of the *Ecclesia Anglicana* to which we have referred, the visit of St Joseph of Arimathea to these shores and of the first Christian King of Britain, Lucius, whose direct descendant now sat upon the throne. Representations of Britons, both tamed and untamed, appear in Speed's *Theatre of the Empire of Great Britain* (1611–12) and Brutus, the first British King, stands on the title-page of Michael Drayton's *Poly-olbion* (1612).[30] Surely this figure is meant to be the Trojan Brutus, founder of the Empire of Great Britain, whose descendant, James I, hailed so often as 'our second Brute and King', was the present reincarnation by dint of this mighty act of Union.

The British group placed to the King's left is complemented by a second group on his right, figures of which we see the faces only. One is the face of a clean-shaven young man, the other face is elderly and bearded. I cannot pretend to offer a solution but I feel certain that these figures belong within the context of ancient Britain revived. One of them should certainly be Lucius, the first Christian King of Britain. Perhaps the other is the British born Constantine, the Roman Emperor who christianized the Empire. Saxl and Gordon's idea that they could represent Charles I and the Duke of Buckingham can surely be discounted.

Ancient Britons

19 Rubens, *A figure perhaps intended as Brutus, King of Britain*

20 *Briton from John Speed's 'Theatre of the Empire of Great Britain'*

21 *Brutus, King of Britain, from Michael Drayton's 'Poly-olbion'*

22 Rubens, *Minerva*

As we have seen, next to the King the figure who is most active in effecting the Union is Minerva-Pallas. She, together with James, appears in all three of the main ceiling panels so that before we proceed any further it would be as well to try and define precisely what her role is. If the child is the infant Great Britain, which, along with Saxl and Gordon, I believe, Minerva-Pallas can hardly also be Britannia. That tradition is a relatively new one, although unquestioned by either Millar or Palme. The earliest representation I can find of Britannia is a back view of her as 'Res-pub[lica] Brytannica' kneeling in supplication to Queen Elizabeth I on the title-page of John Dee's *General and Rare Memorials pertayning to the Perfect Arte of Navigation* (1577). As R. Lightbown and M. Corbett point out, the fact that Dee shows her as a figure in vaguely classical garb means that he probably had the Britannia of Roman coins in mind.[31] William Camden in his *Britannia* (1586) states, 'Britaine is pourtraied sitting upon rocks in womans habit' and in the 1600 edition he illustrates the relevant coins. In both the 1600 and the 1607 editions she appears on the title-page.[32] Anthony Munday must have been thinking of this when he placed her at the top of a mount in the guise of a 'fayre and beautifull nymph' in his Lord Mayor's Pageant for 1604, *The Triumphs of Re-United Britannia*.[33] No one so far makes any equation of her with Minerva-Pallas. Nor is it made in the book which by its title ought to have made it, Henry Peacham's *Minerva Britanna*

30

Britannia

23 *Respublica Britannica from John Dee's 'General and Rare Memorials . . .'*

24 *Britannia from William Camden's 'Britannia'*

25 *Britannia from Michael Drayton's 'Poly-olbion'*

26 *Britannia from Henry Peacham's 'Minerva Britanna'*

(1612), where Britannia is shown in classical clothes holding a regal sceptre. Later in the book she is described at length as Empress of the Isles, wearing an imperial diadem, holding a sword and a triple sceptre, and arrayed in a robe and mantle 'Whereon were wrought, with rarest skill/Faire cities, Castles, Rivers, Woods',[34] in fact close to how she appears on the title-page of Michael Drayton's *Poly-olbion* (1612) published the same year.[35] Nor do any of the court masques, in which Minerva-Pallas frequently figures, suggest any possibility that such an equation was ever made. In these ceiling panels the goddess Minerva-Pallas acts solely as the embodiment of the King's wisdom in action.

Flanking the central panel are two oval ones depicting Virtues vanquishing Vices, one said to be Hercules as 'HEROIC VIRTUES Demolishing ENVY', the other Minerva-Pallas as 'HEROIC CHASTITY Destroying LUST'.[36] Hercules and Minerva-Pallas are complementary figures. Minerva-Pallas appears here attended by her owl bearing a laurel

27 Rubens, *Hercules vanquishes Envy*

28 Rubens, *Minerva vanquishes Ignorance*

The Evils

29 Rubens, *Envy*

30 Inigo Jones, *Headdress for a Fury in 'Salmacida Spolia'*

wreath. The echoes of the symbolism of the last of the court masques is strong, for the owl appears on the proscenium arch of *Salmacida Spolia*. Jones writes in his gloss: 'the bird of Pallas figured for Prudence'. And surely Jones was thinking of those vanquished Vices on the ceiling, one a snaky-haired female and the other a hideous contorted female, when he peopled the stage with snaky Furies as the personifications of opposition to the Crown in the opening tempest scene of the masque:

> *Ascend, ascend, you horrid sullen brood*
> *Of evil spirits, and displace the good!*[37]

For an evening the Vices on the ceiling came to life on stage to be vanquished once more by that 'secret wisdom' which is alone the King's, wisdom of the sort personified by Minerva-Pallas and Hercules.

THE REIGN OF SOLOMON:
THE GOLDEN AGE OF JAMES I

Moving away from the scenes contemplated by Charles I, we come to those directed towards the visitor at the opposite end of the ceiling, focusing on the panel generally referred to as *The Benefits of the Government of James I*. As in the first panel, James is part of a highly dramatic scene. Enthroned within a niche, he makes a grand gesture vanquishing evil figures into an abyss below while his arm moves to protect Plenty, who is clasping a cornucopia and receiving Peace into her arms. The agents of this banishment are Minerva-Pallas, who wields thunderbolt and shield, and Mercury, who uses his caduceus. Above, two winged figures crown the King with the victor's garland of laurel.

Students of style and composition have pointed out the relationship of this scene to treatments, and in particular those by Rubens, of the Last Judgment. James is Christ, of whom Solomon was a type, raising his hand in judgment, drawing to himself the blessed on the left, and watching as Minerva-Pallas, acting as the Archangel Michael, drives the damned into the pit of Hell.

We have already established the Solomonic thread as the all-pervasive one and the allusion here is direct, for James is enthroned in a niche

34

31 Rubens, *The Reign of Solomon: the Golden Age of James I*

32 Rubens, *The Small Last Judgment (detail)*

33 Raphael, *The Solomonic columns in the cartoon 'The Healing of the Lame Man' (detail)*

flanked by the twisted vine columns of the Temple of Solomon. One of these columns in St Peter's, Rome, legend held to have come from the Temple of Jerusalem.[38] The prime source for such columns north of the Alps was, of course, the Raphael Cartoons which were purchased by Charles I and used in the Mortlake tapestry workshops. The initial overall statement is clear. It is James again as the Old Testament Solomonic King. The relationship to his successor below would have been strengthened in that he too sat enthroned in a domed niche.

There are three threatening figures, one an armed man brandishing a torch, the second a nude with snaky hair hurtling backwards, and lastly a many-headed hydra. For the average seventeenth-century Protestant English visitor to Whitehall Palace these could only ever refer directly to two events, the Gowrie Plot of 1600 and the Gunpowder Plot of 1605.[39] Both were transformed into official state festivals, occasions when court clerics and parish clergy alike preached to their congregations on the theme of the iniquity of those who dared raise a hand against the Lord's Anointed and of the terrible results that would befall them. The words in the Prayer Book service for Gowrie Day are not so far different in feeling from what we see: 'Let them be driven backward, and put to rebuke, that wish any evill to his Royall person, or to our gracious Queene, or to any of their most worthy Progenie . . .'[40] But if I had to choose a single text by which to explain this scene of drama and judgment in allegorical terms it would be Ben Jonson's masque *The Golden Age Restored*, danced as part of the New Year's revels of 1615. In this, Pallas arrives in her chariot to carry out Jove's commands, to restore Astraea and to re-establish the Golden Age. Her task, however, is rudely disturbed by an anti-masque of the Iron Age, Insolent Rebellion (in the eyes of James I the ultimate crime against God's vice-regent) attended by Evils. These she turns into statues:

> So change, and perish, scarcely knowing how,
> That 'gainst the gods do take so vain a vow,
> And think to equal with your mortal dates
> Their lives that are obnoxious to no fates.[41]

34 Rubens, *Minerva vanquishes the assailants of the throne*

Jove, the author of this new Golden Age, is of course James I. Let us now return to the Rubens ceiling where James is shown banishing Evils from his presence. As in the masque, his agent is Minerva-Pallas wielding Jove's thunderbolt. She rams away with her Medusa shield a figure which must surely be Insolent Rebellion brandishing his torch. Behind him the other Evils, consisting of the man with the envious snaky hair and the hydra, fall backwards.

In the masque there follows the inevitable resolution. Pallas proceeds to summon the maiden Astraea and the Golden Age to descend: 'But how, without a train/Shall we our state maintain?' they ask in bewilderment. Pallas replies: 'Leave that to Jove [i.e. James I], therein you are/No little part of his Minerva's care.'[42] Spenser, Chaucer, Gower and Lydgate are summoned as witnesses to the fact that 'buried arts will flourish'. The masquers are revealed when 'Pallas throws a lightning from her shield. To which let all that doubtful darkness yield.'[43] And Astraea sums up the theme of the whole courtly spectacle:

> *Of all there seems a second birth;*
> *It is become a heav'n on earth,*
>   *And Jove is present here:*
> *I feel the Godhead! nor will doubt*
> *But he can fill the place throughout,*
>   *Whose power is everywhere.*[44]

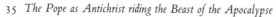

35 *The Pope as Antichrist riding the Beast of the Apocalypse*

36 Paul van Somer, *James I holds up the Garter George on which a Protestant knight vanquishes the Dragon of Rome (detail)*

And the dénouement on the ceiling is the same. James gestures towards the peace and plenty that his wise actions have ushered in.

And what is this Golden Age which James brings in his role as the messianic ruler, that part into which every Renaissance monarch was inevitably cast? Again, as in the case of the Union, it is less political than religious. What Rubens would surely have been kept in ignorance of when presented with the programme was how specifically anti-Catholic the panel was. To most Protestants the hydra was the Pope identified as the Beast of the Apocalypse. And Jones, we know, was reformist. 'And loe, this is now more than the fiftieth year, wherein the people of this lande in abundance of peace sat (as the Prophet saieth) Everyman under his owne vine . . .' Thus sings a cleric in a sermon preached on the King's Accession Day early in the reign.[45] Through this gift to his people he has enabled them to 'live to serve God in Bethel, at IERUSALEM, in the house of God and City of Peace'.

37 Rubens, *Peace embraces Plenty*

38 Rubens, *Mercury vanquishes the assailants of the throne*

In other words the Golden Age is Protestant and reformist and James driving backwards a hydra-head can only refer to Antichrist, the Beast of the Apocalypse, identified by extreme Protestant theologians with the Papacy. The image of the rulers of England vanquishing the hydra-dragon had its place in Tudor and Stuart royalist mythology in glosses on the emblem of the Order of the Garter depicting St George slaying the dragon. Post-Reformation Protestant glosses transform the saint into a sacred emblem designed to incite valiant Garter Knights to vanquish the Roman Antichrist. A Jacobean poem catches the flavour:

> *The Garter is the favour of a King,*
> *Clasping the leg on which man's best part stands;*
> *A poesy in't, as in a nuptial ring,*
> *Binding the heart of their liege Lord in bands;*
> *That whilst the leg hath strength, or arm the power,*
> *To kill that serpent would their King devour . . .*
> *God keep our King and them from Rome's black pen,*
> *Let all that love the Garter say, Amen!*[46]

Following the example of his predecessor James I occasionally holds up the Garter Badge in his portraits as an incitement to the onlooker.

In a sense, therefore, we can look at this panel through Spenserian eyes as the false Duessa vanquished by Una, the pure ancient Christianity embodied in the imperial church of the Empire of Great Britain. How amazing that it is Rubens, the artist *par excellence* of the Catholic Counter-Reformation, who should be painting all this. It is this religious *renovatio* to which James gestures in the Rubens canvas and the agents of his triumph are, as in the court masques, abstract emanations of the royal will and intellect. Minerva-Pallas reappears in her role as regal wisdom, expressed in heroic action that can vanquish foes who threaten the throne just as it can make righteous judgments. Her ally in the victory is Mercury, the god of eloquence and messenger of Jove, who strikes down discord with the

39 *Religion and Peace on the title-page to James I's 'Workes'*

caduceus of concord. Mercury surely represents James in his spoken and
written pronouncements, the learned monarch who is able to instruct his
subjects in the mysteries of his office by speeches to Parliament or the Court
of Star Chamber, or who can defend the cause of the *Ecclesia Anglicana* and
Divine Kingship against the wanton attacks of Catholic and Puritan
alike. In exactly the same way James is glorified on the title-page of his
Workes (1616). A crown of stars is let down from heaven for this erudite
monarch, and Peace and Religion are in attendance. The former also
displays the attributes of Plenty, for she holds the cornucopia as well as
treading underfoot the weapons of discord.[47]

This panel is for the edification of those who, lowly and with heads
uncovered, by means of etiquette and ritual, make their obeisance to him
who sits on the throne. They are told of the gifts of peace and plenty
ushered in by the rule of kings by Divine Right. The theme is expanded

40 Rubens, *Temperance vanquishes Intemperance*

41 *Ripa's 'Ragione'*

42 *Ripa's 'Temperanza'*

in the two panels that flank it, which again depict regal Virtues vanquishing Vice. And these panels for the first time, prompt reference more directly to what is without doubt the key source-book for the iconography of the ceiling, James I's own exposition of monarchy by Divine Right, the *Basilikon Doron*, written for the edification of his son, Henry Prince of Wales. The central theme of this can, for our purposes, be summed up by the opening couplet of the sonnet placed at the very beginning:

> *God gives not kings the style of Gods in vain*
> *For on his throne his Sceptre do they sway . . .*[48]

The *Basilikon Doron* is a book within the *speculum principis* tradition, those mirrors which list the qualities an ideal prince should have; it therefore has a great deal to say about regal virtues. Indeed, the placing of the

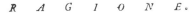

R   A   G   I   O   N   E.   *T   E   M   P   E   R   A   N   Z   A.*

45

Virtues on the ceiling follows the book precisely. Justice, James I writes, is the greatest virtue. She, as we shall see, bears the King to heaven in the central panel of the ceiling. The task of a Prince, according to the *Basilikon Doron*, is principally to 'exercise true Wisedome'. In other words the reference is to Minerva-Pallas, the chief actor in the Union and Golden Age panels. To these James adds the virtues personified in the two side panels, both of which are conceived by him in the Aristotelian sense as means between extremes. The bridle seen in the first side panel is the attribute of Temperance, defined by James as the Queen of the Virtues: '. . . wise moderation, that first commaunding your selfe, shall as a Queene, commaund all the affections and passions of your minde, and as a Phisician, wisely mix all your actions according thereto therefore, not onely in all the affections and passions, but even in your most virtuous actions, make ever moderation to be the chiefe ruler.'[49]

43 Rubens, *Liberality vanquishes Avarice*

44 *Ripa's 'Liberalità'*

45 *Ripa's 'Avaritia'*

The other virtue mentioned by James is Liberality: 'Vse trew Liberalitie in rewarding the good, bestowing frankly your honour and weale: but with that proportionall discretion, that every man may be served according to his measure . . .'[50] In the second side panel Liberality pours forth a cornucopia of riches. Thus the two side panels expand the meaning of the central scene with virtues that are maxims of good government.

These two panels accord perfectly with what we know of Jones's iconographical method as practised not only in devising allegorical figures for the court masques but in designing their costumes. Even in the early masques he would ignore Jonson's directions as to symbolic attribute and insert his own.[51] But by the 1630s he was in absolute control. And Jones's approach was considerably less learned and full of antiquarian zeal than that of Ben Jonson. Jones compiled his figures

L I B E R A L I T A'.

A V A R I T I A.

47

above all from Cesare Ripa's *Iconologia*, the standard artist's manual which he used throughout his career. But he used it in his own particular way, as a quarry into which he dipped, selecting from this and that figure attributes which he then combined into something which had a life of its own. If we turn up *Liberalità* in Ripa we find a woman holding a cornucopia of riches as in the ceiling, but she also supports a cornucopia of fruits and has an eagle on her head.[52] These Jones discounts. For the appearance of the rest of the figure we must look under *Felicità Eterna*, who is described as a young man with golden tresses garlanded with laurel, seated beautiful and resplendent in a starlit sky.[53] Combining a selection of the attributes of these figures from Ripa, we get a scenario on the lines of the wise and just king who, by observing the virtue of liberality to his people, ensures their eternal happiness.

Similarly Temperance with her bridle is a composite image. In the proscenium arch to *Salmacida Spolia*, in which so many of the images on the ceiling are recalled, Jones describes a figure as having '. . . much majesty in her aspect, apparelled in sky colour, with a crown of gold on her head, and a bridle in her hand, representing Reason'.[54] If we look up *Ragione* in Ripa we find a lady with a golden crown bridling a lion. But she also carries a sword in her right hand and has a waistband inscribed with arithmetical figures. From *Ragione* Jones has taken the bridle and the crown.[55] But if we turn to *Temperanza* we find another lady, similar to the one on the ceiling, with a bridle but attended by an elephant.[56] In other words we should be reading this panel as the virtue of regal temperance exercised through reason in governing the kingdom and subjecting Vices.

The Vices on the ceiling are similarly handled. Liberality vanquishes a combination of attributes derived from the five images of *Avaritia* listed by Ripa. Nearly all these images are of hideous women: one woman is bare-breasted and more than one clutches a money bag, which is what the hag on the ceiling seems to be doing. Intemperance is devoid of attributes and the wolf below is attached as an attribute by Ripa to figures as varied as Doubt, Hypocrisy, Avarice, Self-Interest and Voracity.

On either side of the central apotheosis are two narrow strips forming friezes of putti. These move in joyous procession either towards the throne or away from it. In other words their original positioning is arguable. One depicts a triumphal chariot laden with corn, drawn by a wolf and ram harnessed together; the other a second chariot onto which a cornucopia is being emptied and which is drawn by a lion and a bear. These are enriched by a number of other incidents: a putto tames a tiger by riding on its back, another tickles a tiger by the ear, two putti bear up a heavy cornucopia, another draws a lion's teeth while a whole bevy of putti disport themselves amidst the fruits of an immense garland.

The theme is an obvious one and proceeds directly from the previous panel, bringing its Golden Age prognostications to visual fulfilment in the time-honoured Virgilian imagery. Ben Jonson usefully paraphrases these in his masque *The Golden Age Restored* (1615):

> *Then earth unplowed shall yield her crop,*
> *Pure honey from the oak shall drop,*
> *   The fountain shall run milk;*
> *The thistle shall the lily bear,*
> *And every bramble roses wear,*
> *   And every worm snake silk.*[57]

We see here in sportive imagery the fruits of the virtuous rule of James I. Jones, when he directly re-uses this imagery in 1640 for the last of the masques, gives us the gloss. These children expressed 'the several goods, followers of peace and concord, and forerunners of human felicity'.[58]

On the proscenium arch of the masque two incidents were repeated from the ceiling frieze: '. . . winged children, one riding on a furious lion, which he seems to tame with reins and with a bit . . . a third flying over their heads with a lighted torch in his hand, representing the intellectual light . . .'[59] Once again we see the bridled lion of Ripa's *Temperanza*, and if we turn to *Intelletto* in Ripa we find a figure wearing an accumulation of attributes from which Jones has selected a flame of fire and a sceptre.[60]

46 Rubens, *A putto bridles a lion*

47 Rubens, *A putto carries a torch and a sceptre*

48 *Ripa's 'Intelletto'*

The great central oval is the climax of the ceiling and presents James I ascending heavenwards at an astonishingly steep perspective angle on the back of an imperial eagle and globe. He is guided by Justice who bears the scales in her right hand but with her left grasps James firmly by the arm. He looks towards her and she towards him, as though their relationship was something immediate and special. The King in fact does not look heavenwards but steadfastly fixes his gaze on her, the means by which he has achieved his ascent. To his right are two other regal virtues, Religion, eyes cast upwards, carrying an altar aflame with sacrifice, and Faith, clasping the Bible. The other half of the oval is filled by a celestial reception party. Two putti support the King's terrestrial crown while a further group to the right make music with trumpets and carry the victor's palm. Victory, with huge outspread wings, holds a caduceus in one hand while with the other she joins Minerva⁄Pallas in supporting a crown of laurel over the King. Beyond, more putti celebrate the event, bearing a garland of oak leaves, the civic crown, and a sprig of roses.

The apotheosis is the climax to the whole ceiling and in no other part, I believe, is the King's book, the *Basilikon Doron*, followed so closely.[61] Here we have revealed to the visitor below and to the reigning King alike the rewards awaiting a ruler of the *Basilikon* type. Book One of the *Basilikon* is entitled 'Of a King's Christian Duty Towards God' and describes how the prime task of man's service to God is Religion, the lady whom we see to the King's right with her altar (a figure again from Ripa[62]). Knowledge of Religion, we are told, comes through knowledge of the Scriptures, and next to Religion Faith carries a Bible open with the inscription, *In principio erat Verbum*, 'In the beginning was the Word', the opening line of St John's Gospel. The Bible is borne by Faith, and James in the *Basilikon* proceeds from Religion to Faith as 'the nourisher and quickener of Religion', 'the golden chaine that linketh the faithfull soule to Christe'. Faith, he writes, is nourished by prayer, and so we see her here with her face turned upwards in contemplation of the glory of the light of heaven. The Scriptures act as a crucial guide to the

49 Rubens,
The Ascension

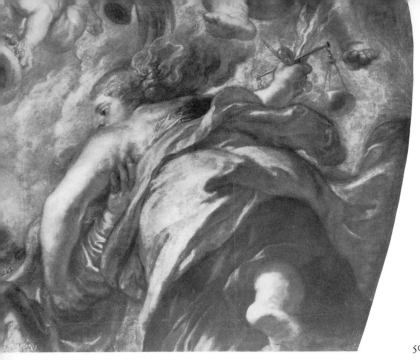

conscience, and James has a long denunciation of papists and puritans who revel in their own fancies as against letting themselves be guided by the purity of the Scriptures. On the ceiling Faith is Protestant, conceived in accordance with the tenets of the Reformation, while in the case of Religion the least Catholic-looking image is drawn from Ripa.

Book Two of the *Basilikon*, entitled 'Of a King's Duty in his Office', deals with Justice and Equity and so our eyes should turn to the right, to the figure lifting the King upwards. Justice and Equity are the key virtues in kingly duty: 'the one, in establishing and executing, (which is the life of the Law), good Lawes among your people: the other, by your behauiour in your owne person, and with your seruants, to teach your people by your example . . .'[63] Justice must be administered to all the estates of the realm impartially. This, in brief, is the burden of the *Basilikon Doron*, with the coda that he who pursues these paths of virtue will go down to posterity as a good king. 'For a good King (after a happie and famous reigne) dieth in peace, lamented by his subjects and admired by his neighbours; and leauing a reuerent renowne behinde him in earth, obtaineth the Crowne of eternall felicitie in heauen.'[64] In this way James prognosticates his own canonization before the event.

An even closer text in the King's own words comes in his *Meditation upon the Lords Prayer.*

'I know not by what fortune, the *dicton* of PACIFICVS was added to my title . . . but I am not ashamed of this addition: for King *Salomon* was a figure of CHRIST in that, that he was a King of peace. The greatest gift that our Sauiour gaue his Apostles, immediatly before his Ascension was that hee left his Peace, with them.'[65]

So the programme for the ceiling reaches its climax and its finale with James I identifying himself through Solomon, the prototype, with Christ making his ascension into heaven, leaving behind the divine gift of peace.

WHITEHALL AND THE TEMPLE OF SOLOMON

One final question. Was there some overall scheme that embraced the whole of the Banqueting House; indeed was there a project even as early as 1619 for rebuilding the whole palace? This is a question which, I believe, has not been raised for a long time, although Palme comes near to it in his view that the ceiling programme existed in earlier versions going back to the 1620s. For an answer we have to shift our minds for a moment away from the Stuart court and seventeenth-century England to the Spanish Habsburg court over half a century earlier and another palace, the Escorial.[66] The architect of the Escorial was Juan de Herrera, one of Spain's leading adepts in the doctrines of Raymond Lull, the thirteenth-century Catalan philosopher. One can make a certain cautious parallel between Jones and Herrera. By 1563 Herrera was assistant to the designer of the Escorial and was versed in mathematics and architecture, had some knowledge of astronomy and mechanics, and was a good draughtsman. He also seems to have been conversant with Italian. In other words he can be placed along with Jones within the tradition of the Vitruvian architect-engineer, a creator of buildings in the new classical style based on Renaissance theories of proportion and symmetry as expressed through number. In 1567 Herrera became personal assistant to the King, Philip II, and was the mastermind behind the creation of the Escorial.

Herrera's intellectual preoccupations place him strongly within the context of Renaissance hermeticism and magic. The magical interpretation of art reaches its climax in two mannerist treatises by Giovanni Paolo Lomazzo, *Trattato dell'Arte della Pittura, Scoltura et Architettura* (1584) (part of which was translated into English by Richard Haydocke) and *Idea del Tempio della Pittura* (1590). Both these handbooks propagated the notion of the artist as the purveyor in action of the *idea*, the inner vision of the creative mind manifesting itself. In the case of the Escorial there was such a single *idea* which governed its whole concept and symbolism. As René Taylor has shown, that *idea* stemmed from the identification of Philip II with Solomon, so that his palace was deliberately built as a recreation of the Temple of Solomon.

We know how this worked through a remarkable publication by Herrera's pupil, the Jesuit, Juan Bautista Villalpando, who published a book in Rome in 1605 entitled *De Postrema Ezechielis Prophetae Visione*, part of a three-volume commentary on the prophet Ezechiel. Three chapters are devoted to the reconstruction of the Temple of Solomon.

51 *The Escorial*

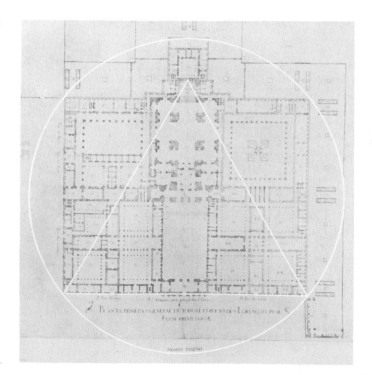

52 *Villalpando's ground-plan of the Temple of Solomon*

53 *The Escorial in relation to the triangle and the circle*

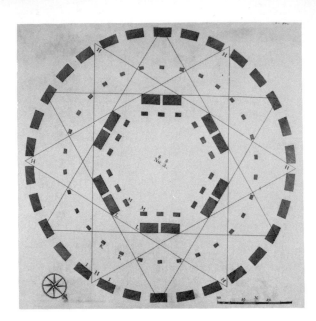

54 *Inigo Jones's plan of Stonehenge*

Villalpando, in tune with the times, manages to harmonize Renaissance classical culture with the Scriptures by turning the Temple into a classical one and arguing that Solomon built it according to Vitruvian principles.

Now let us return to England to examine what was in many ways a parallel situation, a Vitruvian architect-engineer designing a palace for a King who identified himself directly with Solomon. The contents of Inigo Jones's library would never place him so strongly within the magico-hermetic tradition as Herrera but he certainly belongs to it as it existed in England epitomized by the great Elizabethan magus, John Dee. Frances Yates point this out in her study of the architect's extraordinary analysis of Stonehenge, which Jones somehow squares with Vitruvius' plan of an ancient theatre based on four equilateral triangles inscribed within a circle.[67] What is important, as she shows, is not whether Jones is right or wrong but that his study of Stonehenge is the only document we have which shows how his mind worked in relation to the concept or *idea* of a building. Jones argues, often very

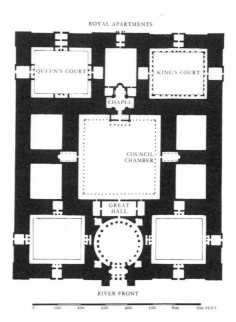

QUEEN'S COURT

KING'S COURT

CHAPEL

COUNCIL
CHAMBER

GREAT
HALL

RIVER FRONT

55 *Plan of a projected new palace*
of Whitehall

0   100   200   300   400   500   600   700 FEET

illogically, that Stonehenge was built by the Romans as a Temple to the
god Coelus, a conclusion he reaches by means of an analysis of the
iconography of the geometry.[68] He looks up a circle in that most famous
of handbooks of Renaissance symbolism, Valeriano's *Hieroglyphica*, and
learns 'not only . . . the circular form, but the mere segment of a circle
amongst the Egyptians was an hieroglyphic of Coelus'. Hence
Stonehenge is a temple to this god, an argument reinforced by the
equilateral triangles, 'the figure', he writes, 'whereby the ancients
expressed what appertained to heaven and divine mysteries'.

Bearing in mind the Escorial and Jones's approach to buildings as
revealed in his study of Stonehenge, let us look at one of the earliest plans
for the rebuilding of Whitehall Palace.[69] These are dated by
architectural historians to the close of the 1630s and without a doubt the
earliest show a layout that could only stem from a familiarity with
Villalpando's reconstruction of the Temple of Solomon. Here are the
same courtyards and the same great central church. In subsequent
drawings the latter disappears, but here in its earliest surviving stages we

59

56 *Villalpando's elevation of the Temple of Solomon*

57 *Elevation of Whitehall Palace*

58 *Whitehall Palace in relation to the triangle and the circle*

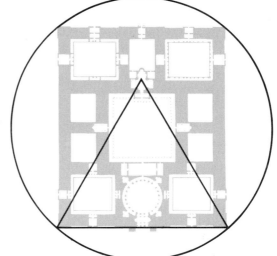

are tapping the *idea* which animated what would have been Jones's greatest architectural monument. Nor perhaps should we ignore the striking resemblance between the engraving of the elevation of the Temple of Solomon and early drawings of about 1638 by Jones's assistant, John Webb, for the river front of the new Whitehall. As a footnote it is fascinating that the copy of Villalpando now in the British Library belonged to the old Royal Library and bears James I's arms on its binding. In addition, when Charles I was imprisoned at Carisbrook Castle he spent his time studying our key book, Villalpando's exposition of the Temple of Solomon.[70] And it was precisely at this period that John Webb was asked by the King to revive the palace project.

The parallels with the symbolic geometry of the Escorial can, I suggest, be taken even further. The palace itself is almost a square and can be embraced within a circle whose radius stems from the centre point of the central courtyard. An equilateral triangle superimposed upon the ground-plan finds its apex in the chancel of the Chapel Royal in exactly the same way as at the Escorial. The full implications of this approach I must leave to architectural historians but just as Stonehenge, as Jones deduced, was made up of astrological figures that succeeding ages might know that it was a temple dedicated to the god Coelus, so the plan of Whitehall Palace was composed of mystical geometry that posterity might know that here lived the Solomonic Kings of Great Britain.

Although this particular late-1630s plan envisaged a new site at St James's and the demolition of the existing Banqueting House (although the Rubens canvases would doubtless have been re-sited in a new ceremonial hall), surely the central *idea* of any new palace must have been at the back of Inigo Jones's mind as early as 1619. Rubens specifically states in his letter, a fact which no one points out although it has been quoted by every historian of the subject, that he had been asked to decorate 'the hall in *the new palace*' (my italics). In other words we must cease thinking that the Whitehall Banqueting House (apart perhaps from its very initial stages) could ever have been conceived in total isolation. It was built with absolutely no concessions to the rambling old Tudor palace, as two façades facing outwards and inwards to the *cour d'honneur*. There were no ends to it. Even in 1622, when it was finished, it stood as the single piece of a vast jigsaw, the remaining pieces of which in the end never came. I cannot support this with either written evidence or drawings, and subsequent schemes, it must be admitted, sometimes envisage its demolition. But what I would like to pose is the hypothesis that the building and the ceiling are the only parts of a vast scheme for a new palace centring on the Solomonic idea and that this was in

59 *Inigo Jones's view of the Whitehall Banqueting House when just finished*

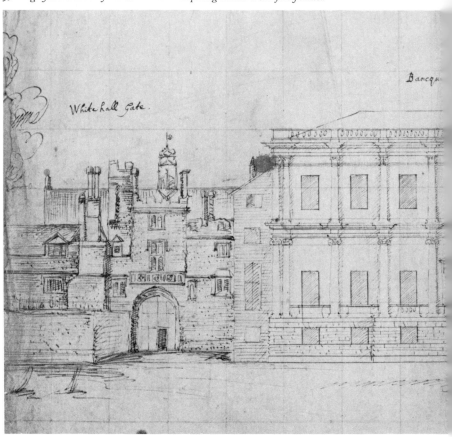

everybody's mind from the first discussions back in James I's reign.[71] Whatever was hammered out in 1629 between Rubens, Charles I and Inigo Jones took place within this overall context, that of Solomon and his Temple.

The iconography of the ceiling is therefore much more than the localized decoration of one room. Here Jones, through Rubens, gives us the vital clue to the meaning of Whitehall Palace as it existed in his mind

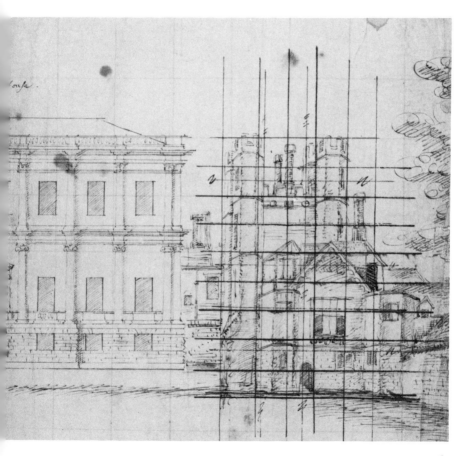

over the decades. It is Jones the Neoplatonist speaking to us, the believer in the architect's supreme role as purveyor in building terms of the harmonic structure of the universe, of macrocosm and microcosm. Throughout his career Jones was also obsessed with fusing old and new, with superimposing the newly recovered harmonious architecture of antiquity onto the Gothic chivalry of ancient Britain. He was also fiercely Protestant, which gives his work a curious twist, one which makes him, for instance, christianize Stonehenge into a temple to Coelus, an argument he surprisingly supports by an analogy to Solomon's Temple: '. . . was not the *Temple* at *Hierusalem* adorned with the figures of *Cherubims*, that thereby the Nations of the Earth might know it was the habitation of the living God? and, why not in like manner this *Temple* composed by *Astrologicall* figures, that after Ages might apprehend, it was anciently consecrated to *Coelus* or *Coelum* Heaven?'[72]

As we stand in the Whitehall Banqueting House today we can still experience all the impulses of such an imagination, as it conceived the *idea* of Whitehall. In Jones's mind ancient Britain revived was also a revival of the ancient British and hence Protestant religion. The recovery of classical architecture with its mirror image of a harmonic universe was for him also the recovery of a Christian architecture, the classical orders sanctified by their use in the Temple of Solomon and by Vitruvius who wrote in the reign of Augustus when Christ was born. Palace and ceiling were meant to be read through numerical, geometric and symbolic allusion as a celebration of the Emperors of Great Britain, those reincarnations of the Old Testament Kings, whose prototype was Solomon. 'Here', proclaimed Bishop Williams at James I's funeral, 'the *Lawes* were iustly administred, here all the *Tribes* were vsually assembled, here the three *Kingdomes* were conuened, here *Edenburgh* and *Diuelen* were vnited like *Iebus* and *Salem*, in one *Hierusalem*. Whilst *Salomon raigned in this Hierusalem*.'[73]

APPENDIX

The only surviving printed key to the Whitehall ceiling exists in the form of a photograph of a lost broadsheet in the Victoria & Albert Museum. It is undated but the date usually assigned to it is the second half of the seventeenth century. Typographically, however, a date about 1820 would seem more likely.

ROYAL BOUNTY Pouring *from a* CORNUCOPIA CROWNS MEDALS *and* Trampling AVARICE *Underfoot.*

KING JAMES *the* FIRST *on the* THRONE Pointing to PEACE *and* PLENTY Embracing MINERVA *and* WISDOM Driving with a Thunderbolt REBELLION *and* ENVY *into* HELL *and* MERCURY laying them *to* SLEEP with his CADUCEUS

GOVERNMENT *with a* BRIDLE TRAMPLING REBELLION *Underfoot.*

A LION DRAWING a CHARIOT *with an* ANGEL *on his* BACK TICKLING HIM in his EAR *and another* DRAWING HIS TEETH, ALLUDING *to the* HARMONY in KING JAMES'S REIGN.

THE APOTHEOSIS *or Translation of the* KING *after* DEATH *the* KING Trampling on the GLOBE *and* Flying on the WINGS *of an* EAGLE JUSTICE lifting *and* CONDUCTING him to HEAVEN attended by RELIGION *and* ZEAL, HONOUR *and* VICTORY CROWNING HIM

BACCHUS RIDING *on a* RAM DRAWING a CHARIOT laden with FRUIT REPRESENTING the PLENTY of KING JAMES'S REIGN.

HERCULES *Representing* HEROIC VIRTUES Demolishing ENVY

the KING on his THRONE Pointing to PRINCE CHARLES *who is* CROWN'D KING [of] SCOTLAND Perfected by MINERVA *or* WISDOM.

PALLAS *or* MINERVA *Representing* HEROIC CHASTITY Destroying LUST.

NOTES

1 For texts and interpretation see S. Orgel and R. Strong, *Inigo Jones. The Theatre of the Stuart Court*, London, 1973, I, pp. 71–2; II, pp. 661 ff.

2 ibid., II, p. 662.

3 W. N. Sainsbury, *Original Unpublished Letters Illustrative of the Life of Sir Peter Paul Rubens*, London, 1859, pp. 59–61; also *The Letters of Peter Paul Rubens*, ed. R. S. Magurn, Cambridge, Mass., 1955, p. 46.

4 Cited in virtually all the studies of the ceiling as listed in note 5.

5 I make no attempt to list here all the literature on Rubens that touches on the ceiling. From the point of view of the study of the iconography of the ceiling the following are the only serious contributions of any importance: Per Palme, *Triumph of Peace. A Study of the Whitehall Banqueting House*, London, 1957, pp. 225 ff.; Oliver Millar, 'The Whitehall Ceiling', in *Burlington Magazine*, XCVIII, 1956, pp. 258–67; idem, *Rubens. The Whitehall Ceiling*, Charlton Lectures on Art, London, 1958; D. J. Gordon, *The Renaissance Imagination*, ed. S. Orgel, Berkeley, 1975, pp. 3–10, 24–50. Also useful for facts is the *London County Council Survey*, XIII, 1930, pp. 121–2.

6 Julius Held, 'Rubens's Glynde Sketch and the Installation of the Whitehall Ceiling', in *Burlington Magazine*, CXII, 1970, pp. 274–81.

7 This scope was comprehensively revealed in the exhibition marking the quatercentenary of Jones's death: See J. Harris, S. Orgel and R. Strong, *The King's Arcadia. Inigo Jones and the Stuart Court*, Arts Council Catalogue, London, 1973.

8 Orgel and Strong, *Inigo Jones*, I, p. 52.

9 ibid., II, p. 483.

10 ibid., II, p. 734.

11 Gordon, *The Renaissance Imagination*, p. 4.

12 See Appendix, p. 65 above.

13 See S. T. Bindoff, 'The Stuarts and their Style', in *English Historical Review*, LX, 1945, pp. 192–216; see also for the treatment of this theme in courtly revels, D. J. Gordon, 'Hymenaei: Jonson's Masque of Union', in *The Renaissance Imagination*, pp. 168–74.

14 *Documents relative to the Reception at Edinburgh of the Kings and Queens of Scotland*, Edinburgh, 1822, pp. 30–1.

15 *The Workes of the Most High and Mighty Prince James . . .*', London, 1616, 'To the Reader'.

16 John Williams, *Great Britains Solomon*, London, 1625. This is based on an exposition of the four Virtues adorning the hearse designed by Inigo Jones: Religion, Justice, Peace and War.

17 John Thornborough, *A discourse plainely prouing the euident utilitie and urgent necessitie of the desired happie Vnion . . .*, London, 1604, p. 15.

18 Charles H. McIlwain, *The Political Works of King James I*, Cambridge, 1918, p. 272.

19 Orgel and Strong, *Inigo Jones*, II, p. 730.

20 Gordon, *The Renaissance Imagination*, pp. 39–40.

21 H. A. Evans, *English Masques*, London, n.d., pp. 1–16.

22 John Thornborough, *The Ioeful and Blessed Reuniting of the two mighty and famous kingdomes, England and Scotland into their ancient name of great Brittaine*, Oxford, 1604 or 1605, pp. 25–6.

23 Orgel and Strong, *Inigo Jones*, I, p. 342 (115).

24 ibid., II, p. 456, ll. 260–72; p. 464 (193).

25 John Gordon, *A Panegyrike of Congratulation for the Concord of the realmes of Great Britaine in vnitie of religion and under one King*, London, 1603, p. 23. He then proceeds with the usual paean on the Emperor Constantine with a parallel to James. This is repeated in the same author's *ENΩTIKON Or a Sermon of the Vnion of Great Britannie ...*, London, 1604: 'The Britaines before all nations first publikely receaved the Faith of Christ ...' Then follows the usual succession of Lucius, Constantine and James. See also *The Triumphs of King Iames the First ...*, London, 1610, p. 88.

26 Samuel Pegge, 'A Dissertation on the Ancient Establishment and Function of the Serjeant at Arms', in *Curialia*, V, London, 1806, p. 24. I am indebted to Mr J. L. Nevinson for this reference.

27 Orgel and Strong, *Inigo Jones*, I, pp. 220–8 (67–71).

28 ibid., I, p. 578, ll.954–8; pp. 590–7 (284–91).

29 John Speed, *History of Great Britaine*, London, 1611, p. 191.

30 On which see M. Corbett and R. Lightbown, *The Comely Frontispiece. The Emblematic Title-Page in England 1550–1660*, London, 1979, pp. 157–8.

31 ibid., p. 54.

32 ibid., p. 155.

33 J. Nichols, *The Progresses of James I*, London, 1828, I, pp. 564 ff.; she also appears in the 1605 Coronation entry as *Monarchia Britannica*, 'a woman richly attired in cloth of gold and tissue; a rich mantle; over her state two crowns hanging, with pencilled shields through them, . . . In her hands she holds a sceptre; on her head a fillet of gold, interwoven with palm and laurel; her hair bound into four several points, descending from her crowns . . .' (I, p. 377).

34 Henry Peacham, *Minerva Britanna 1612*, English Emblem Books No. 5, ed. John Horden, London, 1973, pp. 108, 210. Peacham's book is not unuseful in relation to the ceiling in that many of its emblems are based directly on the *Basilikon Doron*.

35 Corbett and Lightbown, *The Comely Frontispiece*, pp. 153–61. Thornborough, *Ioeful and Blessed Reuniting*, op.cit., uses the image of Pallas riding in triumph as symbolic of the Union but there is no association with Britannia: 'If I could express the image of this union in lively colours, I would surely make her a Goddes, faire, and beautiful, having a garland, & crowne of al blessings vpon her head, & sitting in a Chaire of State with al good fortune, vertues and graces attending her, and as a Goddes in a trumphant chariot going to the capitol, or temple of mighty Iupiter: where also the Poets have found her, but called by another name, euen Pallas, who is also named *Monas* (cites Macrobius), that is unitie: because having one only parent, shee resideth in Iupiters braine, even the chiefe seate of his wisedome . . .' (p. 19).

36 See Appendix, p. 65 above.

37 Orgel and Strong, *Inigo Jones*, II, p. 731, ll. 142–3. For *Invidia* see Cesare Ripa, *Iconologia*, Padua, 1611, pp. 261–2; the Furies in the masque draw also on *Discordia*, p. 121.

38 Elisabeth Rosenbaum, 'The Vine Columns of Old St Peter's in Carolingian Canon Tables', in *Journal of the Warburg and Courtauld Institutes*, XVIII, 1955, pp. 1–15; J. B. Ward Perkins, 'The Shrine of St Peter and its Twelve Spiral

Columns', in *Journal of Roman Studies*, XLII, 1952, pp. 21 ff.; A. Sartario, 'Le Colonne Vitinee e le colonne tortili', in *Rassegna d'Arte*, XII, 1912, pp. 175 ff.

39 Popular literature casts the Gunpowder Plot inevitably in terms of hell-fire and torches: see William Barlow, *A Brand, Titio Erepta* . . ., London, 1607: 'to light a Torch before the Sunne'; 'What fancie, what furie, what Devill could haue so inraged the spirit of any, to haue set seuen *glorious Brandes* on fire, at once to consume them'. Once again the snaky headed Fury appears (see note 37). The hydra in Ripa can refer to Envy, Wickedness, Vice and the Seven Mortal sins (*Iconologia*, pp. 261, 365, 459, 470).

40 *A fourme of Prayer with Thankesgiuing, to be vsed by all the Kings Maiesties louing Subiects euery yeere the fifth of August*, London, 1603.

41 *Ben Jonson: The Complete Masques*, ed. S. Orgel, New Haven, 1969, p. 227, ll. 71–4.

42 ibid., p. 228, ll. 126–7, 128–9.

43 ibid., p. 229, ll. 134–5.

44 ibid., p. 232. ll. 213–18.

45 Richard Crackenthorpe, *A Sermon Preached at the Solemnizing of the Happie Inauguration of our most gracious and Religious Soueraigne KING IAMES* . . ., London, 1609. The theme is inevitably Solomon and there is the usual reference to Constantine.

46 Quoted and discussed in Roy Strong, *The Cult of Elizabeth. Elizabethan Portraiture and Pageantry*, London, 1977, pp. 182–3.

47 Corbett and Lightbown, *The Comely Frontispiece*, pp. 137–42.

48 McIlwain, *The Political Works of James I*, p. 3.

49 ibid., p. 37.

50 ibid., p. 42.

51 See for example Orgel and Strong, *Inigo Jones*, I, p. 379 (130).

52 Ripa, *Iconologia*, pp. 310–11.

53 ibid., p. 167. He also carries a palm and flames which Jones discounts. No one as far as I know has pointed out that this figure must be a man and not a woman.

54 Orgel and Strong, *Inigo Jones*, II, p. 730.

55 Ripa, *Iconologia*, p. 45.

56 ibid., p. 509.

57 *Ben Jonson: The Complete Masques*, ed. Orgel, p. 230, ll. 154–9.

58 Orgel and Strong, *Inigo Jones*, II, p. 730.

59 ibid., loc.cit.

60 Ripa, *Iconologia*, pp. 257–8.

61 Gordon was the first to point this out, *The Renaissance Imagination*, pp. 37–8.

62 Ripa, *Iconologia*, p. 458: 'Matrona, d'aspetto venerabile, vestita di panno di lino bianco; terrà la destra mano aperta, & la sinistra sopra van'altare, nel quale arderà fiamma di fuoco . . .' Palme points this out, *Triumph of Peace*, p. 246, n.2.

63 McIlwain, *The Political Works of James I*, p. 18.

64 ibid., p. 19.

65 *The Workes of the Most High and Mighty Prince, James* . . ., London, 1616, 'Meditation upon the Lords Prayer' (this section of the *Workes* was published in 1620).

66 For what follows see René Taylor, 'Architecture and Magic. Considerations of the *Idea* of the Escorial', in *Essays in the History of Architecture Presented to Rudolf Wittkower*, ed. D. Fraser, H. Hibbard and M. J. Levine, London, 1967, pp. 81–109, and *idem*, 'Hermeticism and Mystical Architecture in the Society of Jesus', in *Baroque Art. The Jesuit Contribution*, ed. R. Wittkower and I. B. Jaffe, New York, 1972, pp. 63–91 (especially pp. 73–81 on Villalpando and the Temple of Jerusalem). See also Helen Rosenau, *Vision of the Temple. The Image of the Temple of Jerusalem in*

Judaism and Christianity, London, 1979, where the influence of Villalpando is traced. In England, Hollar's illustrations for the *Biblia Sacra Polyglotta* (1657) are simplified copies of Villalpando.

67 Frances A. Yates, *Theatre of the World*, London, 1969, pp. 80–91.

68 S. Orgel, 'Inigo Jones on Stonehenge', in *Prose*, III, 1971, pp. 109–24.

69 Margaret Whinney, 'John Webb's Drawings for Whitehall Palace', in *Walpole Society*, XXXI, 1946, pp. 45–107. See also John Summerson, *Inigo Jones*, London, 1966, pp. 127 ff.; Harris, Orgel and Strong, *The King's Arcadia*, pp. 146–7.

70 Sir Thomas Herbert, *Memoirs of the Two last Years of the Reign of that unparallell'd Prince, of ever blessed Memory, King Charles I*, London, 1702, pp. 42–3. I am indebted to C. V. Wedgwood for this reference.

71 The old belief was always that the Banqueting House was the fragment of a much larger scheme *ab initio*. This was first demolished by J. Alfred Gotch, 'The Original Drawings for the Palace at Whitehall attributed to Inigo Jones', in *The Architectural Review*, XXXI, 1912, pp. 333 ff. Evidence published by E. S. de Beer made it clear that a palace project was in hand in the late 1630s, a fact accepted by both Whinney and Summerson. The latter accepts what she designates the **P** series of drawings as the only ones done directly under Jones's direction. No one seems to make use of Rubens's well-known letter of 1621 which refers to the 'new palace'. See also Harris, Orgel and Strong, *The King's Arcadia*, pp. 129–30.

72 Inigo Jones, *The Most Notable Antiquity of Great Britain vulgarly called Stonehenge . . .*, London 1655, p. 107.

73 Williams, *Great Britains Solomon*, p. 62.

LIST OF ILLUSTRATIONS

Collection Viscount Hampden, Glynde Place. Photo Sydney W. Newbery.

10 Rubens, *The Judgment of Solomon: James I recreates the Empire of Great Britain*. Painting. Panel from the Whitehall Banqueting House ceiling. Photo Department of the Environment.

11 Daniel Mytens, *James I (detail)*, 1621. Painting. National Portrait Gallery, London.

12 Rubens, *Putto setting light to armour and weapons. Detail from 'The Judgment of Solomon: James I recreates the Empire of Great Britain'.* Painting. Panel from the Whitehall Banqueting House ceiling. Photo Department of the Environment.

13 Inigo Jones, *Design for 'Masque of Augurs'*, 1622. Drawing. Devonshire Collection, Chatsworth.

14 Rubens, *Serjeant at Arms. Detail from 'The Judgment of Solomon: James I recreates the Empire of Great Britain'.* Painting. Panel from the Whitehall Banqueting House ceiling. Photo Department of the Environment.

15 Inigo Jones, *Design for Oberon in 'Oberon, the Fairy Prince'*, 1611. Drawing. Devonshire Collection, Chatsworth. Photo Courtauld Institute, University of London.

16 Inigo Jones, *Design for a torchbearer or attendant in 'Oberon, the Fairy Prince'*, 1611. Drawing. Devonshire Collection, Chatsworth.

17 Inigo Jones, *Design for a masquer as an ancient British hero in 'Coelum Britannicum'*, 1634. Drawing. Devonshire Collection, Chatsworth.

18 Inigo Jones, *Design for a torchbearer in the 'old British fashion' in 'Coelum Britannicum'*, 1634. Drawing. Devonshire Collection, Chatsworth.

19 Rubens, *Detail of the figure here identified as Brutus, King of Britain, from 'The Judgment of Solomon: James I recreates the Empire of Great Britain'.* Painting. Panel from the Whitehall Banqueting House ceiling. Photo Department of the Environment.

20 *Ancient Briton from John Speed's 'Theatre of the Empire of Great Britain'*, 1611–12. Engraving by Jodocus Hondius. Photo British Library.

21 *Brutus, King of Britain. Detail from the title-page to Michael Drayton's 'Poly-olbion'*, 1612. Engraving by William Hole.

22 Rubens, *Minerva. Detail from 'The Judgment of Solomon: James I recreates the Empire of Great Britain'.* Painting. Panel from the Whitehall Banqueting House ceiling. Photo Department of the Environment.

23 *Respublica Britannica from the title-page to John Dee's 'General and Rare Memorials pertayning to the Perfect Arte of Navigation'*, 1577. Wood-engraving by an unknown artist.

24 *Britannia from the title-page to William Camden's 'Britannia'*, 1607. Engraving. Photo British Library.